COMMITTEE ON COMMERCE, SCIENCE, AND TRANSPORTATION

BILL NELSON
RANKING MEMBER

Children's Connected Toys: Data Security and Privacy Concerns

OFFICE OF OVERSIGHT AND INVESTIGATIONS
MINORITY STAFF REPORT

DECEMBER 14, 2016

Table of Contents

Executive Summary

This holiday shopping season, millions of parents will consider purchasing "smart" toys for their children. These "connected toys" – toys that are connected to the Internet – offer many promising applications, including the potential to assist in the overall education and cognitive development of children. The personally identifiable information (PII) collected by these connected toys, however, also raises serious privacy and data security concerns. These concerns are magnified when the data at issue is sensitive children's information.

The improper disclosure of a child's personal information – including, for example, name, home address, online contact information, or physical location – can lead to inappropriate contact, sexual exploitation, or abduction. In addition to clear physical threats, children's personal information is a growing target for identity thieves. Bad actors can use children's information to create false identities that can be used to engage in a variety of financial frauds and other crimes.

Unfortunately, there have been a number of instances in which companies offering connected toys and devices have failed to adequately secure the information they collect from or about children. Last year, a hacker accessed the consumer data collected by VTech Electronics North America, LLC (VTech), a manufacturer of connected tablets for children. The VTech breach exposed the data of more than six million children and four million parents worldwide – 2.8 million children and 2.2 million parents in the U.S. – including children's names, genders, dates of birth, and photographs. Additionally, researchers found security vulnerabilities associated with two other child-directed connected devices – the Fisher-Price Smart Toy Bear and KGPS hereO GPS watch.

Following these incidents, Ranking Member Nelson sent letters to these three companies – VTech, Fisher-Price, and KGPS – requesting more information about the incidents and the companies' data privacy and security policies. To more fully assess the data security and privacy practices in the connected toy industry, Ranking Member Nelson also sent letters to three other major manufacturers of children's connected devices asking about their data collection, use, and security.

The responses from these six companies provide the basis for this report. The toymakers' responses revealed that connected toys collect a variety of information, including PII, both from the child and parent. The responses also indicated that toymakers have data security policies in place to protect collected consumer data. However, the VTech breach as well as the Fisher-Price Smart Toy Bear and hereO watch security vulnerabilities reveal that some toymakers have failed to secure collected consumer data. These incidents raise troubling questions regarding whether connected toymakers are adequately prioritizing the security of the information they collect from children.

The growth in connected toys has created not only valuable benefits for parents and children but also significant privacy and security risks. To mitigate these risks, toymakers, the Federal Trade Commission (FTC), and parents should take the following steps:

- **Toymakers should build in effective security from a connected toy's inception:** Due to the sensitivity of children's data, toymakers should build connected toys with security as a top priority from the toy's inception. Investment in robust security and continued updates to security measures are critical. Toymakers should also implement reasonable data privacy practices, including collecting only data that is required for the core functions of the toy and retaining collected information for only as long as it is necessary. Furthermore, they should use clear, plain language to inform parents about the information the toys collect and how that information is used.

- **The FTC should carefully monitor the evolving connected toy space:** As the federal regulator that enforces the Children's Online Privacy Protection Act and Section 5 of the FTC Act, the FTC should carefully monitor the connected toy space and exercise its authority when appropriate. In addition, as the country's principal consumer protection agency, the FTC should continue to protect the privacy and security of consumers' personal information.

- **Parents should understand the data privacy and security risks that accompany connected toys:** As toys become even more sophisticated, it is imperative that parents are aware of the privacy and security risks associated with connected toys. Parents should:
  - See what personal information the toy will collect, how that information will be used, whether it will be shared, and how long the information will be retained. Often this information is addressed in the toy's privacy policy. If the toymaker has a long and confusing privacy policy, or if parents determine that the toy collects too much personal information, parents may want to reconsider giving that product to their child.
  - Check whether the toymaker has been the subject of a prior data breach and how that breach was handled. In particular, parents can check whether the company offered any remedial measures after the breach, such as credit monitoring services.
  - Change default passwords that come with the toy to strong, unique passwords and install any available updates to the toy's software.
  - Change privacy settings, if possible, to limit the amount of personal information provided to the toymaker. Allow the toy to only collect the information necessary for the toy to properly function.

I. Introduction

The dramatic increase in the number of Internet-connected devices comprising the so-called "Internet of Things" has created numerous benefits for consumers. For example, "smart" thermostats in the home can improve energy efficiency and wearable technology can monitor a user's health and fitness. In recent years, children's toys have evolved from simple, stuffed teddy bears to "connected toys" – toys that are connected to the Internet and can talk to and interact with children. Last year, it was estimated that connected toys were a $2.8 billion industry.[1]

At the same time, however, the collection and use of personal data through connected devices raise important privacy and data security concerns. These concerns are magnified when the data at issue is particularly sensitive, such as children's personal information. As a result, makers of connected toys and other smart devices designed primarily for use by children must ensure that they have in place robust privacy and security measures that effectively protect the data they collect. Unfortunately, as toys have become "smarter" and more prevalent, some connected toymakers have failed to implement sufficient data security practices.

Last year, a hacker accessed the consumer data of VTech Electronics North America, LLC (VTech), a maker of children's connected tablets.[2] The VTech breach exposed the data of more than six million children and four million parents worldwide, including children's names, genders, and birthdates, as well as photographs and account passwords.[3] Additionally, security vulnerabilities associated with two other connected devices for children – Fisher-Price Inc.'s (Fisher-Price) Smart Toy Bear and KGPS Ltd.'s (KGPS) hereO GPS watch – were reported this year. These devices suffered from basic security flaws that could have exposed highly sensitive information, including, in the case of the GPS watch, children's real-time physical locations.[4]

---

[1] *Smart Toy Revenues to Hit $2.8BN This Year, Driven By Black Friday & Christmas Holiday Sales*, Juniper Research (Nov. 9, 2015) (online at https://www.juniperresearch.com/press/press-releases/smart-toy-revenues-to-hit-$2-8bn-this-year).

[2] *One of the Largest Hacks Yet Exposes Data on Hundreds of Thousands of Kids*, Motherboard (Nov. 27, 2015) (online at http://motherboard.vice.com/read/one-of-the-largest-hacks-yet-exposes-data-on-hundreds-of-thousands-of-kids) (hereinafter "Motherboard VTech Article").

[3] *Id. See also FAQ About Cyber Attack on VTech Learning Lodge*, VTech (Aug. 8, 2016) (online at https://www.vtech.com/en/press_release/2016/faq-about-cyber-attack-on-vtech-learning-lodge/).

[4] *R7-2015-27 and R7-2015-24: Fisher-Price Smart Toy® & hereO GPS Platform Vulnerabilities (FIXED)*, Rapid7 (Jan. 25, 2016) (online at https://community.rapid7.com/community/infosec/blog/2016/02/02/security-vulnerabilities-within-fisher-price-smart-toy-hereo-gps-platform) (hereinafter "Rapid7 Fisher-Price Smart Toy & hereO GPS Platform Vulnerabilities Report"). In addition, Mattel's Wi-Fi enabled Hello Barbie was also found to have a security vulnerability. *See Hackers Can Hijack Wi-Fi Hello Barbie to Spy on Your Children*, The Guardian (Nov. 26, 2015) (online at https://www.theguardian.com/technology/2015/nov/26/hackers-can-hijack-wi-fi-hello-barbie-to-spy-on-your-children).

II. Children's Personal Information Is Particularly Sensitive and a Growing Target for Identity Thieves

In the United States, children's personal information is considered sensitive data, and Congress has afforded it heightened protection by law.[5] This approach is consistent with the treatment of other types of sensitive personal information, including financial and health data, where the repercussions of the information falling into the wrong hands can be dire.[6] With respect to children's data, the improper disclosure of a child's personal information – including, for example, name, home address, online contact information, or actual location – could lead to inappropriate contact, sexual exploitation, or abduction. While these threats are not unique to children, given the vulnerability of this population, the potential for harm is substantially increased.

In addition to clear physical threats, bad actors can use children's information to create false identities that can be used to engage in a variety of financial frauds and other crimes. The Federal Trade Commission (FTC) notes that identity thieves can use a child's Social Security number "to apply for government benefits, open bank and credit card accounts, apply for a loan or utility service, or rent a place to live."[7] Thieves can also use pieces of personal information in "phishing" schemes – schemes in which information already acquired is used to trick a victim into revealing additional personal data.[8]

A number of factors make children a particularly attractive target for identity thieves. A child's identity is a "blank slate" that can be fraudulently used over a long period of time without detection.[9] Parents generally do not monitor their children's credit histories and thus may not know for years that an identity thief has victimized their child.[10] Personal information about children may also be more readily available as children and parents often fail to

---

[5] *See* The Children's Online Privacy Protection Act of 1998, 15 U.S.C. §§ 6501-6508.

[6] *See* The Health Insurance Portability and Accountability Act of 1996, 42 U.S.C. § 1320d-6; Gramm-Leach-Bliley Act of 1999, 15 U.S.C. § 6801.

[7] Child Identity Theft, Federal Trade Commission (Aug. 2012) (online at https://www.consumer.ftc.gov/articles/0040-child-identity-theft).

[8] *See, e.g., Hack of Toy Maker VTech Exposes 5 Million Customers*, CNET (Nov. 27, 2015) (online at https://www.cnet.com/news/hack-of-toy-maker-vtech-exposes-families/) ("Hackers can use stolen data for a range of phishing attacks designed to target people through their email addresses and get them to click on links that trigger malicious software which lets the hackers steal even more sensitive information.").

[9] *See* Federal Trade Commission, Prepared Statement of the Federal Trade Commission before House Committee on Ways and Means, Subcommittee on Social Security (Sept. 1, 2011) (online at https://www.ftc.gov/sites/default/files/documents/public_statements/prepared-statement-federal-trade-commission-child-identity-theft/110901identitythefttestimony.pdf).

[10] *See, e.g., Cyberthieves Have a New Target: Children*, The Wall Street Journal (Jan. 31, 2016) (online at http://www.wsj.com/articles/cyberthieves-have-a-new-target-children-1454295685).

appreciate the potential consequences of sharing this information through social media or connected toys and devices.

A number of studies indicate that large numbers of children in the United States are victims of identity theft. A study by ID Analytics, a consumer risk management company, estimated that more than 140,000 children are victimized each year.[11] A 2011 Carnegie Mellon study of 40,000 children enrolled in an identity protection service determined that 10.2% had someone else using their Social Security numbers – 51 times the rate for adults.[12] Further, a 2012 study by AllClear ID, an identity protection and credit monitoring service, indicated that children are 35 times more likely than adults to be victims of identity theft and that the rate of identity theft among children under the age of five had more than doubled.[13]

III. Statutory Protections for Children's Personal Information

Depending upon the specific context, two federal laws enforced by the FTC could apply to the collection of personal information through connected toys and other devices intended for use by children.

a. Children's Online Privacy Protection Act

The Children's Online Privacy Protection Act (COPPA)[14] gives parents control over the information that is collected online from their children. COPPA applies to operators of websites or online services that are directed to children and to operators of general audience sites or services that have knowledge they are collecting information from a child.[15] Before a covered operator collects personal information[16] from a child younger than the age of 13, the operator must provide the child's parents with notice about the operator's data collection and use practices and obtain verifiable parental consent.[17] In addition, the operator must take steps to "protect the confidentiality, security, and integrity of personal information collected from

---

[11] *More Than 140,000 Children Could Be Victims of Identity Fraud Each Year*, ID Analytics (July 12, 2011) (online at http://www.idanalytics.com/blog/press-releases/140000-children-victims-identity-fraud-year/). ID Analytics noted that, due to limitations in its study, this figure likely under-represented the actual rate of child identity theft.

[12] Carnegie Mellon CyLab, *Child Identity Theft*, at 9 (2011) (online at https://www.cylab.cmu.edu/files/pdfs/reports/2011/child-identity-theft.pdf).

[13] *Child Identity Theft Report 2012: What to Know*, (May 1, 2012) (online at https://www.allclearid.com/personal/2012/05/child-id-theft-report-2012/).

[14] 15 U.S.C. §§ 6501-6508. The FTC enforces the law through 16 C.F.R. Part 312 ("COPPA Rule").

[15] *See* Complying with COPPA: Frequently Asked Questions, Federal Trade Commission (Mar. 2015) (online at https://www.ftc.gov/tips-advice/business-center/guidance/complying-coppa-frequently-asked-questions).

[16] The COPPA Rule defines personal information to include: first and last name; home or other physical address; online contact information; telephone number; Social Security number; Internet Protocol address; photos, videos, or audio files containing a child's image or voice; and geolocation. 16 C.F.R. § 312.2.

[17] 16 C.F.R. §§ 312.4-312.5.

children."[18] If the operator transfers children's personal information to a third party, the operator must also ensure that the third party has taken similar steps to protect the data.[19]

Accordingly, a connected toy or device that is designed to collect personal information from a child could trigger COPPA's requirements of parental notice, consent, and reasonable data security. If a toymaker violates these COPPA requirements, it can be fined up to $40,000 per violation.[20]

b. Section 5 of the Federal Trade Commission Act

Section 5 of the Federal Trade Commission Act (FTC Act) directs the FTC to protect consumers from "unfair methods of competition" and "unfair or deceptive acts or practices in or affecting commerce."[21] The FTC has used its broad Section 5 authority over unfair or deceptive acts or practices to protect the privacy and security of consumers' personal data. For example, when a company misrepresents its practices regarding the type of personal information it collects or the way it uses or safeguards this data, the misrepresentation could constitute a deceptive act that violates Section 5.[22] In addition, even absent such a misrepresentation, when a company's data practices (1) cause or are likely to cause substantial injury to consumers; (2) that the consumer cannot reasonably avoid; and (3) that is not outweighed by countervailing benefits to consumers or competition, the practices may be "unfair" and therefore violate Section 5.[23]

In the context of children's toys, a maker of a connected device that collects children's information could violate Section 5 of the FTC Act if it misrepresents its data collection and use practices. Even without a misrepresentation, if the toymaker fails to adequately protect the data it collects and uses, that failure could be "unfair" and therefore a potential violation of Section 5.

IV. Ranking Member Nelson's Investigation

Following media reports in November 2015 of a data breach at VTech that potentially exposed the personal information of millions of parents and children,[24] Ranking Member

---

[18] 16 C.F.R. § 312.8.

[19] *Id.*

[20] Federal Trade Commission, *Adjustment of Civil Monetary Penalty Amounts*, 81 Fed. Reg. 42476 (June 30, 2016) (interim final rule).

[21] 15 U.S.C. § 45(a)(1).

[22] *See* Federal Trade Commission, FTC Policy Statement on Deception (Oct. 14, 1983) (online at https://www.ftc.gov/public-statements/1983/10/ftc-policy-statement-deception).

[23] 15 U.S.C. § 45(n).

[24] Motherboard VTech Article, *supra* note 2; *When Children Are Breached – Inside the Massive VTech Hack*, Troy Hunt (Nov. 28, 2015) (online at https://www.troyhunt.com/when-children-are-breached-inside/).

Nelson sent a letter to VTech requesting information about its data privacy and security practices and its plans to address the vulnerabilities that led to the breach.[25] To better understand the data privacy and security practices of other connected toymakers, Ranking Member Nelson also sent letters to three other major manufacturers of connected children's tablets: Fuhu, Inc., KD Group, and LeapFrog Enterprises, Inc.[26] The letters asked a series of questions about the types of information the companies' products collect, with whom they share the information, and the security measures the companies have in place to protect the collected information – especially information about children – against a breach.

Following a report in early 2016 that two additional children's devices – KGPS' hereO GPS watch and Fisher-Price's Smart Toy Bear – potentially had serious security vulnerabilities,[27] Ranking Member Nelson sent letters to these companies requesting information about their data collection, use, and security practices – both before and after the discovery of the alleged vulnerabilities.[28] Information provided to the Senate Commerce Committee by these six makers of connected devices and toys for children formed the basis for this report.

V. Information Collected by Connected Toys

Children's connected toys may collect a variety of information, including personally identifiable information, from both the child and parent. While different toys collect different types of data, the total universe of information collected by the toymakers surveyed by Ranking Member Nelson includes:

---

[25] Letter from Ranking Member Bill Nelson to VTech Electronics North America, LLC (Dec. 16, 2015).

[26] Letters from Ranking Member Bill Nelson to Fuhu, Inc., KD Group, and LeapFrog Enterprises, Inc. (Dec. 16, 2015).

[27] Rapid7 Fisher-Price Smart Toy & hereO GPS Platform Vulnerabilities Report, *supra* note 4.

[28] Letter from Ranking Member Bill Nelson to Fisher-Price, Inc. (Apr. 7, 2016); Letter from Ranking Member Bill Nelson to KGPS Ltd. (Apr. 7, 2016). In its response, Fisher-Price explained that all responsibility for data collection and security resides with Smart Toy, LLC pursuant to a license agreement. Smart Toy, LLC is no longer in business, but some of its assets, including technology responsible for the Smart Toy bear's operation, were acquired by Sphero, Inc. (Sphero). *See* Letter from Fisher-Price to Ranking Member Bill Nelson (June 3, 2016). In light of this information, Ranking Member Nelson sent a letter to Sphero. *See* Letter from Ranking Member Bill Nelson to Sphero (Aug. 4, 2016). Although the Information regarding the security of the Fisher-Price Smart Toy bear is based on the response provided to Ranking Member Nelson by Sphero, at the time the security vulnerability existed, Smart Toy, LLC – not Sphero – was responsible for the security of the Smart Toy bear. *See* Letter from Sphero to Ranking Member Nelson (Sept. 16, 2016).

Information Collected About Children	Information Collected About Parents
Birthdate	Email address
Name	Gender
Gender	Profile picture
Profile picture	Chat messages sent by parent
Chat messages sent by child	Voice messages sent by parent
Voice messages sent by child	Photos sent by parent
Photos sent by child	Password for account with toymaker
Password for account with toymaker	Password retrieval question and answer
Geolocation	Mailing address
Call logs	Credit card information
Internet history	Phone number
	Wi-Fi password
	IP address

Connected toymakers may also track information related to the specific ways in which the child interacts with and uses the toy. For example, one toymaker explained in its response to the Committee that "information is collected from, or about, the child such as the types of games that the child plays, websites that they view, videos that they watch, music that they listen to, and their preferences." Depending on how the connected toys are used, the companies may also collect information from additional sources. For example, one toymaker explained in its response to the Committee that "if a parent chooses to access third-party services (such as Facebook or Twitter) through our website, then we may collect information from these third-party services."

The toymakers surveyed by Ranking Member Nelson generally explained that they do not sell the information they collect to third parties. Instead, the companies only share information with third-party service providers, including, for example, payment processors acting on behalf of the toymaker.

While the companies spell out in their privacy policies the information they collect from both a child and parent, studies have shown that most consumers do not actually read or understand these documents. In fact, one study found that more than half of Americans do not know what a privacy policy is.[29] This raises concerns about the extent to which parents are aware of the variety of information that toys may be collecting about their children.

---

[29] Pew Research Center, *Half of Online Americans Don't Know What a Privacy Policy Is* (Dec. 4, 2015) (online at http://www.pewresearch.org/fact-tank/2014/12/04/half-of-americans-dont-know-what-a-privacy-policy-is/); *See*

VI. Data Security Measures and Data Retention Policies of Connected Toymakers

The responses provided by the connected toymakers indicate that toymakers have in place data security measures to protect collected information. These security measures include data retention policies that vary widely in length of time based on the type of collected information.

a. Connected Toymakers' Security Measures

All surveyed connected toymakers have implemented security controls to protect collected data. Generally, the surveyed connected toymakers employ some or most of the following security measures:

Encryption
Firewalls
User restrictions, access controls, and authentication procedures
Remote access through an encrypted VPN tunnel
Monitoring networks for unauthorized activity
Regular updates and patches to software
Vulnerability testing
Engaging independent security services to test systems for vulnerabilities

b. Connected Toymakers' Data Retention Policies

According to the five toymakers that responded to Ranking Member Nelson's questions regarding data retention policies, the length of time the toymakers retain collected data varies widely. One toymaker broadly explained that it "retain[s] personal information only for as long as it is necessary for the purposes for which it was collected." Another toymaker stated that it retains "general data" until the account is terminated or the consumer requests that the data be deleted. The same toymaker keeps location data for 60 days and then automatically deletes it.[30] For its children's tablets, a third toymaker retains information for ten years, with all "sensible [*sic*] information" being "completely hashed before sav[ing]."

Another toymaker, which offers a chat message feature for parents and children, stores these messages only until they are opened by the recipient and then deletes them. Any unopened messages are stored for 30-40 days before they are deleted. Voice messages and photos sent through the chat feature are encrypted and stored for one year.[31] Data collected

---

also Why Privacy Policies Are So Inscrutable, The Atlantic (Sept. 5, 2014) (online at http://www.theatlantic.com/technology/archive/2014/09/why-privacy-policies-are-so-inscrutable/379615/).

[30] KGPS Response, at 4.

[31] VTech Response, at 6 (Jan. 22, 2016).

from this toymaker's service that allows parents to download apps, learning games, and other educational content is "stored as long as the parent maintains an active account."[32]

VII. **The VTech Breach and Fisher-Price Smart Toy Bear and hereO Watch Security Vulnerabilities Suggest Toymakers May Not Be Adequately Securing the Information Collected from Children**

In certain instances, toymakers have failed to adequately secure collected consumer data, including information about children. The recent VTech breach, as well as the vulnerabilities found in the security of the Fisher-Price Smart Toy bear and hereO GPS watch, raise troubling questions regarding whether connected toymakers are adequately prioritizing the security of the information they collect from children.

a. VTech Breach

VTech manufactures children's tablets and phones and also provides an online store, called Learning Lodge, where parents can download e-books, learning games, and apps for VTech devices. VTech also offers Kid Connect, a service that allows parents and children to exchange voice messages, text messages, and photographs between a smartphone app and VTech tablet.[33] In November 2015, VTech experienced a massive data breach that raised new concerns about the security of children's connected toys. At the time of the breach, VTech's products and services collected the following consumer data:

- Parent account information including: name, email address, secret question and answer for password retrieval, IP address, mailing address, download history, history of device purchases, and profile photo
- Child profile information including: child's name, gender, birthdate, and profile photo
- Chat and voice messages sent by children and parents
- Photos sent by children and parents[34]

All of this data was potentially compromised in the November 2015 breach when a hacker reportedly accessed VTech's database by using an SQL injection, a technique that was described as "an ancient, yet extremely effective, method of attack where hackers insert malicious commands into a website's forms, tricking it into returning other data."[35] The hacker then had full authorization access to databases that stored the personal data and pictures of

---

[32] VTech Response, at 6 (Jan. 22, 2016).

[33] Communicate in Real Time: VTech Kid Connect, VTech (online at https://www.vtechkids.com/brands/brand_view/innotab_max/kid_connect) (last accessed Nov. 18, 2016).

[34] *FAQ About Cyber Attack on VTech Learning Lodge*, VTech (Aug. 8, 2016). VTech states that their databases did not include credit card numbers, debit card numbers, ID card numbers, Social Security numbers, or drivers license numbers. *Id.*

[35] Motherboard VTech Article, *supra* note 2.

millions of parents and children.[36] The breach potentially affected more than 6.4 million child profiles and 4.8 million parent accounts worldwide – 2,894,091 of the child profiles and 2,221,863 of the parent accounts were registered in the United States.[37]

Figure 1: VTech Tablets

This breach exposed VTech's outdated and inadequate security practices. For example, passwords associated with the millions of email addresses were "hashed" with MD5, an algorithm that scrambled user passwords, but MD5 has been criticized as being weak and "trivial to break."[38] According to one security expert, "it's about the next worst thing you do next to no cryptographic protection at all."[39] VTech also failed to "salt" consumers' passwords – a common practice of adding random values to passwords to make them more secure – before hashing them.[40] Furthermore, VTech stored password-reset questions in plaintext, meaning a hacker could have used this readily available information to reset passwords to other accounts belonging to VTech users.[41] It was also observed that VTech did not use SSL web encryption,[42] so all communications, including personal information and passwords, were transmitted over unencrypted connections.[43]

---

[36] *VTech Hacker Explains Why He Hacked the Toy Company*, Motherboard (Dec. 2, 2015) (online at http://motherboard.vice.com/read/vtech-hacker-explains-why-he-hacked-the-toy-company).

[37] *FAQ About Cyber Attack on VTech Learning Lodge*, VTech (Aug. 8, 2016). Additionally, the breach affected 235,708 parent and 227,705 child accounts in Planet VTech worldwide. *Id.*

[38] Motherboard VTech Article, *supra* note 2.

[39] *When Children Are Breached – Inside the Massive VTech Hack*, Troy Hunt (Nov. 28, 2015).

[40] *Id.*

[41] Motherboard VTech Article, *supra* note 2.

[42] *Id* ("SSL is a technology used to protect data sent between a user and a website, and it's typically visualized with a green lock on the URL bar.").

[43] *Id*; *When Children Are Breached – Inside the Massive VTech Hack*, Troy Hunt (Nov. 28, 2015).

Fortunately, the hacker reportedly had no intention of publishing or selling the data.[44] Nevertheless, the breach reveals the potentially significant consequences for millions of consumers, including children, when a single company fails to prioritize the security of the data it collects.

Following the November 2015 data breach, VTech implemented a new data security policy that focuses on "key administrative, technical, and procedural security measures, including data security governance, best practices, awareness and training, and incident response."[45] VTech addressed the security loopholes exposed by the breach by hashing passwords using a stronger algorithm and adding a salt value. VTech also no longer uses secret questions for password recovery, and all data transmitted to VTech servers is protected by SSL encryption.[46]

b. Fisher-Price Smart Toy Bear Security Vulnerability

Figure 2: Fisher-Price Smart Toy Bear

The Fisher-Price Smart Toy bear is a Wi-Fi-connected stuffed animal marketed as "an interactive learning friend that talks, listens, and 'remembers' what your child says and even responds when spoken to."[47] The Smart Toy bear app and web services collect a range of consumer information, including: parent email address and login password; child's first name, birthdate, and gender; toy name and identifier; Wi-Fi password; and mobile device information. The bear itself also gathers information, including images and audio that are stored locally on the toy.[48]

In January 2016, Rapid7, a cybersecurity firm, discovered a security vulnerability associated with the Smart Toy bear. Rapid7 alleged that "many of the platform's web service (API) calls were not appropriately verifying the 'sender' of messages, allowing for a would-be attacker to send requests that shouldn't be authorized under ideal

---

[44] *VTech Hacker Explains Why He Hacked the Toy Company*, Motherboard (Dec. 2, 2015). VTech also has not found any evidence that the hacker distributed the information that he accessed during the breach to anyone other than the Motherboard reporter. VTech Response, at 2 (Apr. 15, 2016).

[45] VTech Response, at 3 (Apr. 15, 2016).

[46] VTech Response, at 4-5 (Apr. 15, 2016).

[47] Smart Toy® Bear, Fisher-Price Shop (online at http://fisher-price.mattel.com/shop/Product2_10151_10101_18442_-1) (last accessed Oct. 27, 2016).

[48] Sphero Response, at 3-4.

operating conditions."[49] In theory, according to Rapid7, this vulnerability could have allowed an attacker to access the Smart Toy server and view children's profiles – including name, birthdate, and gender – as well as details about the parent that registered the toy.[50] Further, an attacker allegedly could have changed a consumer's account and re-associated the toy to a different account – essentially enabling an attacker to "hijack the device's functionality" and "effectively force the toy to perform actions that the child user didn't intend, interfering with normal operation of the device."[51]

After Fisher-Price and Smart Toy LLC – the company providing the technology platform for the Smart Toy bear – learned of the security vulnerability, the companies stated that they resolved the issue within a week.[52] Fisher-Price also had an independent third party verify that the vulnerabilities were fixed, and to the best of Fisher-Price's knowledge, this vulnerability did not directly affect any consumers.[53]

c. **hereO Watch Security Vulnerability**

Figure 3: hereO GPS Watch

---

[49] Rapid7 Fisher-Price Smart Toy & hereO GPS Platform Vulnerabilities Report, *supra* note 4; *Vulnerability Note VU#719736: Fisher-Price Smart Toy Platform Allows Some Unauthenticated Web API Commands*, CERT/CC (Feb. 2, 2016) (online at https://www.kb.cert.org/vuls/id/719736).

[50] Rapid7 Fisher-Price Smart Toy & hereO GPS Platform Vulnerabilities Report, *supra* note 4. However, according to Sphero's response, the Rapid7 report and corresponding CERT/CC note overstated some of the implications of the vulnerability. Rapid7 reported that an attacker would have been able to gain access to a child's full name; however, according to Sphero, an attacker would only have been able to gain access to the child's first name. In addition, according to Sphero, Rapid7 stated that "an attacker would only have needed to create an account in order to take advantage of the vulnerability using their account credentials to acquire information about other users, when in fact that attacker would also have needed to discover the API authentication credentials on the Plush Toy Software in order to do so." Sphero Response, at 2.

[51] Rapid7 Fisher-Price Smart Toy & hereO GPS Platform Vulnerabilities Report, *supra* note 4.

[52] Fisher-Price Response, at 3.

[53] Fisher-Price Response, at 2-3.

In December 2015, Rapid7 disclosed a security vulnerability to KGPS, the maker of the hereO watch – a GPS watch for children that allows parents to track their child's location.[54] The watch utilizes an app that notifies families when a family member arrives or departs from a specific location and allows family members to communicate through the app by sending messages or initiating a panic alert.[55]

Rapid7 found an authorization flaw in the platform's web service that related to account invitations to a family's group.[56] Due to the vulnerability, an attacker allegedly could have requested authorization to join a random family's group and then accepted the request on the family's behalf. The attacker then could have accessed every family member's active location, including the real-time location of a child wearing the watch, as well as the child's location history over time.[57] The vulnerability also could have been used to target other platform features. According to the security research manager at Rapid7, anyone could "basically impersonate the parents, which is creepy." He continued, "Not super useful for traditional computer crime but is definitely in the creepy zone."[58]

KGPS stated that it fixed the security vulnerability within four hours of learning about it.[59] KGPS also added that is has taken additional measures "to improve the product security."[60]

VIII.   Recommendations

The growth in connected toys has created valuable benefits for both parents and children. However, connected toys also pose certain privacy and security risks that, if exploited, could have lifelong impacts for affected children.

Today's smart toys can collect a range of information, including a child's name, gender, birthdate, and location – as well as store a child's pictures, text messages, and audio recordings. The potential risks are only expanding as both the prevalence and sophistication of these toys continue to grow. As the breach of VTech demonstrated, the failure by a single company to adequately secure its data can have serious implications for millions of children and

---

[54] Rapid7 Fisher-Price Smart Toy & hereO GPS Platform Vulnerabilities Report, *supra* note 4.

[55] Meet hereO: The Smallest, Coolest GPS Watch for Children, KGPS Ltd (www.hereofamily.com) (last accessed Oct. 27, 2016).

[56] Rapid7 Fisher-Price Smart Toy & hereO GPS Platform Vulnerabilities Report, *supra* note 4.

[57] *Id.*

[58] *A GPS Tracker for Kids Had a Bug That Would Let Hackers Stalk Them*, Motherboard (Feb. 2, 2016) (online at http://motherboard.vice.com/read/a-gps-tracker-for-kids-had-a-bug-that-would-let-hackers-stalk-them).

[59] *Id.* At the time the vulnerability was exposed, no devices were commercially available. *See also Hackers Could Have Turned Vulnerable Smart Teddy Bear Into Demon Toy*, Forbes (Feb. 2, 2016) (online at http://www.forbes.com/sites/thomasbrewster/2016/02/02/fisher-price-hero-vulnerable-to-hackers/#10e7b9e21cfe).

[60] *A GPS Tracker for Kids Had a Bug That Would Let Hackers Stalk Them*, Motherboard (Feb. 2, 2016).

their parents. Therefore, toymakers, the FTC, and parents should take responsive actions to protect the privacy and security of children.

a.   Toymakers Should Build in Effective Security from a Connected Toy's Inception

The VTech breach, along with the other two cases cited above, must serve as a wake-up call to all makers of connected toys. Other connected toys on the market today may be vulnerable to data breaches, but hackers have not targeted them because they have not yet determined how to monetize the data collected by the toys.[61] This means companies should build in security from a product's inception and invest in technology that ensures that they are always a step ahead of increasingly sophisticated hackers. As the VTech breach clearly demonstrated, basic and outdated security methods will not thwart these dynamic threats.

Toymakers should also limit the amount of data they collect to only that which is required for the core functions of the toy. In addition, retaining collected consumer information for only as long as it is necessary for the toy to operate will reduce the amount of data that is at risk in the event of a breach. Toymakers should also disclose in plain language the information that is collected from or about a child instead of burying it in their privacy policies.[62] Lengthy privacy policies that contain technical language that is difficult to understand are confusing and ineffective. Instead, companies should clearly and definitively explain how they use collected information and avoid open-ended or vague statements that are simply designed to insulate the company from liability.

Furthermore, as discussed above, most consumers do not actually read privacy policies.[63] Providing the basics of what information is collected and how it is used conspicuously and in clear terms – for example, on a toy's packaging – would allow parents to be more informed about their children's privacy and security. This, in turn, will empower them to make better decisions about what toys to buy and how to use them.

Moreover, data security can be a moving target as threats change over time. Companies should frequently reevaluate their practices and security measures to ensure that they are up to date and adequately protecting the consumer information that is collected. The FTC publishes a variety of resources that detail best practices for businesses and discuss how

---

[61] *Toymakers are Tracking More Data About Kids – Leaving Them Exposed to Hackers*, Washington Post (Nov. 30, 2015) (online at https://www.washingtonpost.com/news/the-switch/wp/2015/11/30/toymakers-are-tracking-more-data-about-kids-leaving-them-exposed-to-hackers/).

[62] For example, the VTech privacy policy is almost seven printed pages long. While the beginning of the privacy policy includes a hyperlink to the section that discusses what information is collected from children, this section is located in the middle of the privacy policy – in section 7 of 15. *See* VTech, Privacy Policy (online at https://www.vtechkids.com/privacy_policy/) (last accessed Nov. 17, 2016).

[63] *See* discussion *supra* at Section V.

companies can reduce the risk of a data breach and minimize the impact of a breach if one occurs.[64]

b. The FTC Should Carefully Monitor the Evolving Connected Toy Space

The FTC is the country's principal consumer protection agency, and protecting the privacy and security of consumers' personal information has long been a priority. In addition to its law enforcement authority under a number of sector-specific privacy statutes, as well as its Section 5 authority, the FTC hosts workshops, issues reports, and engages in consumer and business education activities. These efforts frequently focus on emerging technologies or new business models that collect and use consumer data.[65] Given the particularly sensitive information at issue in the evolving connected toy space, the FTC should closely monitor this area and, when appropriate, use its various tools to ensure that consumers are adequately protected.

c. Parents Should Understand the Data Privacy and Security Risks That Accompany Connected Toys

Parents should be aware of the information a toy is collecting about them and their child. While most parents are not data privacy or security experts and therefore may not be in a position to evaluate a company's policies regarding data collection and use, parents should nevertheless make efforts to learn about the ways in which a toymaker collects, uses, and secures data – and reject connected toys that do not provide this information. Parents should:

- See what personal information a toy will collect, how that information will be used, whether it will be shared, and how long the information will be retained. Often this information is addressed in the toy's privacy policy. If the toymaker has a long and confusing privacy policy, or if parents determine that the toy collects too much personal information, parents may want to reconsider giving that product to their child.
- Check whether the toymaker has been the subject of a data breach and how that breach was handled. In particular, parents can check whether the company offered any remedial measures after the breach, such as credit monitoring services.
- Change default passwords that come with the toy to strong, unique passwords and install any available updates to the toy's software.
- Change privacy settings, if possible, to limit the amount of personal information provided to the toymaker. Allow the toy to only collect the information necessary for the toy to properly function.

---

[64] *See, e.g., Start with Security: A Guide for Business*, Federal Trade Commission (June 2015) (online at https://www.ftc.gov/tips-advice/business-center/guidance/start-security-guide-business).

[65] *See, e.g.,* Federal Trade Commission, *Internet of Things, Privacy and Security in a Connected World, FTC Staff Report* (Jan. 2015) (online at https://www.ftc.gov/system/files/documents/reports/federal-trade-commission-staff-report-november-2013-workshop-entitled-internet-things-privacy/150127iotrpt.pdf).

IX. **Conclusion**

     Connected toys have many promising applications with the potential to assist in the overall education and cognitive development of children. At the same time, however, the data privacy and security risks associated with these toys require toymakers to craft and implement comprehensive data protection policies. Regulators must also keep an eye on this evolving connected toy space and ensure that the personal information of parents and children collected by these toys is protected. In the meantime, parents should remain vigilant by selecting connected toys with strong data protection practices to ensure their children's information is safe.